Can the Earth Cope?

Climate Change

Richard Spilsbury

WAYLAND

First published in 2008
by Wayland
Copyright © Wayland 2008
This paperback edition published by Wayland in 2012.

Wayland
338 Euston Road
London NW1 3BH

Wayland Australia
Level 17/207 Kent Street
Sydney NSW 2000

Commissioning editor: Jennifer Sanderson
Consultant: Steph Warren (BA, PGCE, GCSE Principal Examiner)
Designer: Jane Hawkins
Picture researcher: Kathy Lockley
Illustrator: Ian Thompson
Proofreader: Susie Brooks

Picture Acknowledgements:
The author and publisher would like to thank the following agencies for allowing these
pictures to be reproduced: AFP/Getty Images: 35; Dan Anderson/epa/Corbis: 26; ©Arup 44;
G. Bowater/Corbis: 19; Clouds Hill Imaging Ltd/Corbis: 37; Ashley Cooper/Corbis: 25; Tim
Davis/Corbis: 42; Hans Dieter Brandl: Frank Lane Picture Agency/Corbis: 28; Digital
Vision/Getty: Cover main and top left, 8, 11, 34; Doc-stock/Corbis: 20; Martyn Goddard/
Corbis: 38; David Gray/Reuters/Corbis: 6; Momatiuk-Eastcott/Corbis: 12; Jai Redman/CCA
32; Paul Souders/Corbis: 1, 22; USGS, photo by Dave Harlow: 15; Visuals Unlimited/Corbis:
29; Lawson Wood/Corbis: 4

British Library Cataloguing in Publication Data Spilsbury, Richard, 1963-
    Climate change. - (Can the Earth cope?)
    1. Climatic changes - Environmental aspects - Juvenile literature
    I. Title
    577.2'2

ISBN: 978 0 7502 6926 1

Printed in China

Wayland is a division of Hachette Children's Books,
an Hachette UK company.
www.hachette.co.uk

Contents

Changing Climates

Weather can change during the day and from day to day, or it can remain constant for weeks on end. It has a major impact on what people do, from industries, such as farming, to sporting events. However much weather changes, there are limits to how much it usually varies. For example, in the United Kingdom it is never as cold as it can be in Greenland, and never as hot as it can be in the Sahara. The climate of any place is the average pattern of weather, such as the amount of rainfall or sunshine through the year, over long time periods of 30 years or more.

- Ice sheets are up to 4 kilometres thick.
- The polar ice caps contain 2 per cent of the Earth's water.
- During the last ice age 30 per cent of the Earth was under ice.

Past Climates

The climate in different parts of the world has become hotter, colder, drier or wetter over millions of years. There are lots of sources of evidence about past climates. For example, ancient paintings of elephants in water found in caves in the Sahara show that this desert was once a much wetter place. Remains of palm trees and other plants and animals that live only in hot climates have been found frozen in Antarctic ice. Remains of coral reefs have been found inland in Florida, USA. These were once submerged when sea levels were higher because less of the Earth's water was frozen at the Poles.

Ice Ages

Most places on Earth have experienced ice ages in the past. These are periods when the climate is so cold that vast ice sheets and slow-moving, heavy rivers of ice, or glaciers, cover the land. Much of North America, northern Europe, parts of Asia, Australia and New Zealand were under ice from about 2 million until 20,000 years ago. Since then, the ice has melted as the climate has warmed. Glaciers leave tell-tale signs that remain after they have melted. As they move downhill, glaciers scour out valleys with U-shaped cross-sections. They leave piles of rock pieces that they have worn away and pushed in front of them and stones frozen in the sides of glaciers leave scratches on rocks that they pass.

Global Temperatures

Scientists often describe climate change in terms of the rise or fall of average global temperature relative to today. Some climates become much cooler or much hotter and others change by much less, so it is easier to work out an average of all these data. Comparing records of the coldest and hottest average global temperatures reveals differences of only around 10 degrees Celsius. This does not seem to be much, but the last ice age, with sea levels tens of metres lower than today, had an average temperature only 3 degrees Celsius lower than today's.

Coral reefs, such as these in the Bahamas, are in danger of dying when sea temperatures rise. Changing climate is a threat to this ecosystem.

Speeding Up

The speed at which average temperatures change has varied throughout history, but in the past, most changes appear to have been very gradual. For example, it took around 15,000 years for the global average temperature to rise to today's levels after the last ice age. There is evidence though, that climate is changing faster today than at any time in the past. The global average temperature rose by nearly 1 degree Celsius from 1880 to 2006.

This has caused change in many climates. For example, there has been rapid melting of the Arctic ice sheet, and many glaciers on mountains around the world are disappearing. Many scientists believe that the rising temperature is causing more extreme weather events. For example, three of the six most powerful hurricanes in history happened in 2005. Some animals, such as disease-spreading mosquitoes, are shifting into new areas that are now warm enough for them to live in.

▲ Australia is the world's driest continent, and it is getting even drier after several years of drought. Irrigation will be impossible from this empty dam on an Australian farm.

Why Climate Change is Accelerating

The fast rise in average temperatures globally has happened since the start of industrial development over 150 years ago. The rise in production of goods using machine power and the availability of powered transport, from trains to aeroplanes, was based on cheap energy made from coal, oil and other fossil fuels. Fossil fuels are the buried remains of living things that changed over millions of years into resources that people burn to release energy. Industrial development has allowed recent generations to have luxuries their ancestors would not have imagined, ranging from mass-produced goods to leisure time owing to the mechanisation of jobs.

However, this development has come at a cost. Burning fossil fuels releases gases, including carbon dioxide (CO_2), into the atmosphere. Since the end of the 19th century, scientists have been aware of the link between the amount of CO_2 in the atmosphere and how much heat it traps. The increase in fuel use is therefore a major reason why climate is changing. Can the Earth cope with its changing atmosphere? And what can people do to reduce climate change?

Evidence

MELTING PERMAFROST

A small temperature rise is sometimes easier to spot in cold places. In both Siberia and Alaska, near the Arctic, some of the soil is permanently frozen all year round. Some of the permafrost melts each summer. However, the amount that melts is increasing because the average Arctic temperature has risen about by 3 degrees Celsius over the last 50 years. As more permafrost melts, the ground is becoming softer. Houses and roads built on the formerly hard ground are sinking, and the meltwater is forming new lakes.

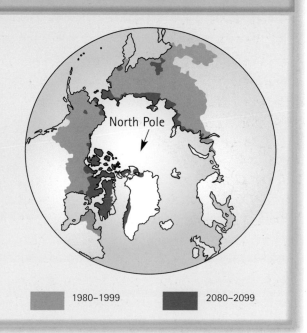

North Pole

1980–1999   2080–2099

The Lowdown on Climate

Climate is caused by interaction between the atmosphere and the Earth's surface. This interaction is driven by energy in rays from Earth's nearest star, the Sun.

Forming Clouds

Clouds, bringing rain and other forms of precipitation, develop in the atmosphere following evaporation of water from rivers, lakes and oceans. Water vapour rises into the atmosphere, cools and condenses into water droplets that form clouds. The energy for the change of state from liquid to vapour comes from sunlight. Sunlight directly warms the water, jiggling the surface water molecules, or warms air masses to create winds that evaporate water, too.

Heat Source

The average temperature at any location on Earth depends on how much of the Sun's heat it receives. This varies partly because Earth is ball shaped and has a curved surface. The Sun's rays move in straight lines to hit Earth most directly at places on the Equator. This is an imaginary line around the middle of the globe. The rays hit the Poles at a slanting angle so heat is spread over a wider area. This is why the Poles are cold.

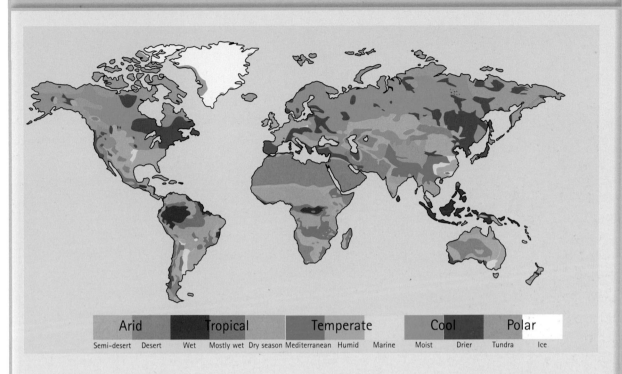

Arid		Tropical		Temperate			Cool		Polar	
Semi-desert	Desert	Wet	Mostly wet	Dry season	Mediterranean	Humid	Marine	Moist	Drier	Tundra	Ice

CLIMATE ZONES

Different parts of Earth can be divided up into several general climate zones. Arid zones have little rain, and are hot throughout the year. Tropical zones are broadly wet and hot all year round. Temperate zones have warm summers and cold winters. Cool zones have severe winters and mild, short summers. Polar zones are freezing and dry through the year.

◀ Winds are air movements caused by air temperature differences. They blow from high pressure, colder air masses to lower pressure, warmer air masses.

However, Earth is not static relative to the Sun. It rotates on an imaginary Pole-to-Pole axis once a day. This creates different temperatures at day and night because different sides are facing the Sun at any time. Earth also orbits, or moves around, the Sun in an oval path that takes a year to complete. The tilt of Earth's axis relative to the Sun means that different parts are closer or further away at different times of year, and this causes seasons. Seasons are not very variable in places on the Equator or at the Poles because these regions are always closest or furthest from the Sun. However, seasons in areas between the Poles have quite different summers and winters.

Trapping Heat

When sunlight reaches Earth, almost a third of the energy is reflected back into space by clouds and particles floating in the atmosphere and by the Earth's surface. The rest is absorbed by and warms up the surface. Heat is then produced from the warm Earth and radiates into the atmosphere. Some heat continues to space, but some is absorbed by clouds and by gases in the atmosphere, including CO_2, methane and nitrous oxide. These gases then radiate some of the heat to space, but most radiates back to Earth. This is the major warming process for the Earth.

The Greenhouse Effect

The atmosphere acts a little like the glass on a greenhouse that lets through sunlight and then reflects back some of the escaping heat and traps it in the greenhouse. This is why this atmospheric process is called the greenhouse effect. The greenhouse effect is vital for life on Earth as it regulates temperatures in all climate zones. Without it, the average temperature on Earth would be -18 degrees Celsius rather than 15 degrees Celsius.

▼ Gases in the atmosphere moderate global temperatures by trapping heat from our nearest star, the Sun.

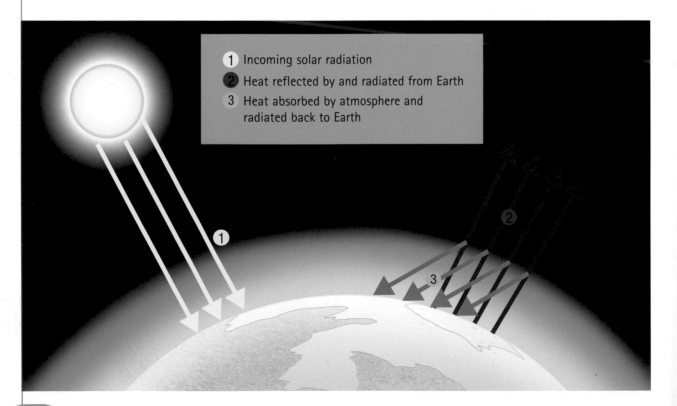

1 Incoming solar radiation
2 Heat reflected by and radiated from Earth
3 Heat absorbed by atmosphere and radiated back to Earth

Surface Effects

The ability of the Earth's surface to reflect or absorb solar radiation depends on what it is like. For example, ice sheets, snow and white buildings are light-coloured and reflective. They absorb less energy than dark, deep water or wooded areas. This is called the albedo effect. Albedo is one reason why ice sheets and glaciers can remain cold. The good heat absorption of concrete, roads, pavements and other materials keeps cities warmer at night than surrounding countryside. This is called the heat-island effect.

The shape and position of the land also affects warmth. As altitude increases, temperature drops because the air gets less dense and less able to warm up. This is why the tops of mountains are so cold. Aspect describes the way land is facing. This also affects surface temperatures. For example, a slope on one side of a valley that has sunlight shining on it all day will be warmer than the other, shaded slope.

▲ Rock at the edge of Antarctica absorbs more heat than the ice.

Evidence

GREENHOUSE CULPRITS

The gases that are most common in the atmosphere, oxygen and nitrogen, are poor at storing heat. Greenhouse gases are those that are better at storing heat. Carbon dioxide is the most common greenhouse gas. There is around 300 times less methane in the atmosphere than CO_2, but this gas can store heat 25 times better. Hydro-Fluoro-Carbons (HFCs) are rare gases in the atmosphere that can store heat 12,000 times better than CO_2. Water vapour is also a greenhouse gas.

The Climate System

Little of the heat energy thay warms places on Earth stays put. Some of it is distributed by winds. For example, air warmed at the Equator rises, carrying water vapour, cools and creates the heavy rain that is typical of tropical climates. The drier, colder winds high in the atmosphere move north or south from the Equator and sink. Cool air then blows from high- to low-pressure areas back to the Equator, where it warms up.

Ocean currents distribute some heat energy. For example, currents warmed in tropical or equatorial areas of ocean move towards and cool in polar oceans. They sink because the water is colder, saltier and therefore more dense than warm water. The deep currents circulate back to warmer places where they rise.

▲ Ocean circulation transports not only heat but also nutrients through the water. In the Antarctic ocean in summer, rising nutrients provide food for plankton. These in turn feed large numbers of krill, which are the shrimp-like animals on which whales feast.

Biomes

A biome is a typical natural landscape plus the community of living things that have adapted to it. Climate is one of the main factors affecting any biome. Animals and plants are often adapted to, or have special features that help them to survive in, particular environmental conditions. For example, polar bears have thick fur to keep warm in the polar climate and the fur is white for camouflage against the white snow and ice as the bears hunt.

Many scientists distinguish six major world biomes: freshwater, marine (or saltwater), deserts, grasslands, forests and tundra. Water is a major limiting factor on life in each. For example, trees, which dominate forests, need wetter climates to grow than grasses, which dominate grassland. Each major biome can be subdivided based on other climate features such as temperature. For example, deserts can be hot or cold. The Sahara is a desert because it receives very little rainfall. Antarctica is a desert because all available water there is frozen and largely unavailable to living things.

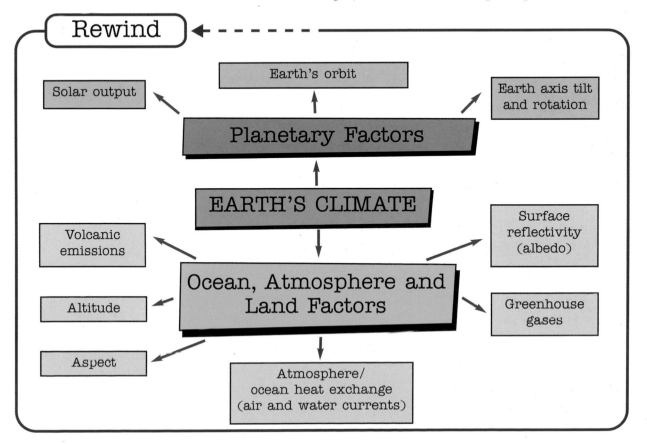

What Causes Climate Change?

Climate change can be caused by natural factors ranging from the changing distance of Earth from the Sun over time to volcanic eruptions that release greenhouse gases into the atmosphere. However, a majority of scientists believe that the changes that people are making to the atmosphere are causing a bigger and more rapid change.

Orbital Theory

Some people believe that much of the climate change the planet has experienced can be explained by regular variations in Earth's orbit around the Sun. The orbit path of the planet changes gradually from an ellipse (oval) to a circle and back to an ellipse every 100,000 years. During this time, the amount of sunlight reaching Earth varies by one-fifth because Earth becomes closer to or further from the Sun. Records of temperature change through history show that the last eight ice ages have fallen in line with the 100,000-year cycle. There are other cycles of

Evidence

RECORDED IN ICE

Whenever snow falls, settles and turns to ice, it traps air bubbles from the atmosphere. In very deep ice sheets or glaciers formed over centuries, yearly layers of ice produce a record of the climate. Scientists use drills to remove long ice cores, sometimes several kilometres in length, in 5-metre-long sections. They analyse the proportions of greenhouse gases in the air inside the bubbles in each section. They also measure the proportion of a substance called deuterium in the ice. The amount of deuterium present reveals how warm and wet the climate was in the past.

41,000 and 26,000 years for Earth's rotational axis that also change its distance from the Sun. These explain patterns in intensity of weather events such as seasonal monsoon rains and warm and cold periods on Earth. The patterns in climate caused by orbital variation are often called Milankovitch cycles after the scientist who worked on them.

Earth Changes

Changes to the structure of Earth also have an impact on climate. The Earth's surface is made up of rock plates floating on hot, liquid rock beneath. Over long timescales the plates have drifted or changed position. For example, about 400 million years ago all of today's continents were bunched together around the Equator and had warm climates. Since then, through continental drift, some areas such as Antarctica, northern Russia and Canada are now located close to or over the Poles.

Volcanic Eruptions

Volcanoes can change climate, too. When they erupt, volcanoes release vast quantities of ash particles and gases into the atmosphere. The particles act as sunblock for the land below, and sulphur dioxide reacts with water vapour in the atmosphere to form a sun-shielding layer. These effects can reduce the temperature for periods lasting several years. However, the volume of greenhouse gases released from volcanoes each year increases the heat absorption of the atmosphere over a longer timescale.

◀ When Mount Pinatubo in the Philippines erupted in 1991, global temperatures dropped by up to 1 degree Celsius for a year afterwards.

The Carbon Age

Human activities since around 1850 have rapidly increased the amount of CO_2 in the atmosphere. This phase in history has been based on making power by releasing energy from burning fossil fuels. At first, machines burned coal largely to heat water and make steam that turned the wheels of anything, from steam trains to cotton-spinning machines in factories. From the early 20th century, people used coal, oil and gas to make electricity to power electrical machines, and oil to run engines in cars, trains, boats and planes. The domestic demand for electricity has risen since the 1950s as technologies, from electric lights and ovens to televisions and computers, have spread globally.

Population

The changes during the carbon age have happened as the world population has rocketed. Since 1850, the global population has increased from just over 1 billion to over 6 billion people. The activities of greater numbers of people have caused increased emissions of greenhouse gases. However, the responsibility for emissions is not evenly spread amongst the global population. An average person in a more economically developed country (MEDC) generally emits much more than someone in a less economically developed country (LEDC). This is the result of using more power and transport. For example, the United States has just 5 per cent of the world's population, yet has emitted around 30 per cent of the total greenhouse gases produced by humans since 1850.

Tipping the Carbon Balance

The quantity of CO_2 produced by human activities is minor compared with that produced by other atmospheric sources. Living things, from whales to bacteria, emit much bigger quantities of CO_2 when they breathe and break down waste. However, green plants on land, soil organisms, and tiny plant-like phytoplankton in the oceans use up CO_2 during photosynthesis.

IT'S A FACT

- Today atmospheric CO_2 is rising 200 times faster than at any point in the previous 650,000 years.

- An average person in the United States emits 20 tonnes of CO_2 each year, 40 times higher than an average person from Senegal.

- Human activities emit 100 times more CO_2 than volcanoes do each year.

Scientists estimate that one-quarter of all carbon dioxide entering the atmosphere is absorbed by phytoplankton, and another quarter by organisms on land.

There is a balance between the amount of CO_2 the natural world produces and how much it absorbs again. Emissions by people tip the balance because they produce more CO_2 than absorbers can remove. The problem is made worse because CO_2 is very persistent. It can remain in the atmosphere for up to 200 years, much longer than any other greenhouse gases. Therefore, each year's emissions add to those of previous years and increase the greenhouse effect.

Evidence

CARBON DIOXIDE AND INCREASING TEMPERATURE

Before 1850, when industries using fossil fuels increased, the CO_2 concentration in the atmosphere was about 277 parts per million. That means there were 277 CO_2 molecules in every million air molecules. Since around 1880, the CO_2 concentration has risen. Today it is 380 parts per million. The lower graph shows how global temperature has risen from 1960–1991 as average levels in the CO_2 concentration has increased. It proves a link between the two.

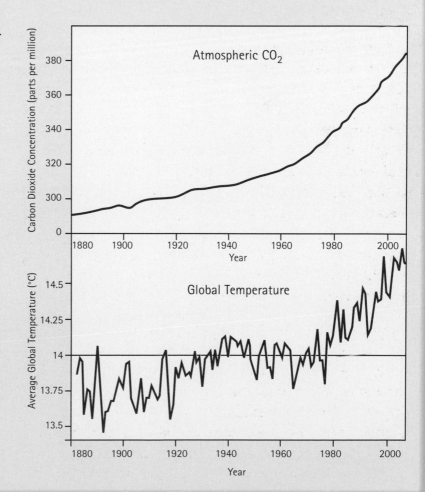

Industrial Emissions

Over one-third of all human-caused greenhouse gas emissions come from powerplants, factories for making goods and from the construction industry. Of these, the power industry is the worst offender because of the demand for power in buildings, from homes to offices. Emissions caused by heating systems, air conditioning and power-hungry electrical machines are rising by 2 per cent each year.

In fast-industrialising LEDCs, such as China and India, emissions are growing quickly. This is partly because coal is their main source of fuel for industry. More greenhouse gases are emitted per unit of energy produced when coal is burned than when other fossil fuels are used. In MEDCs, such as USA, Australia and Japan, industrial emissions are growing more slowly because less coal is being burned now than in the past. The main reason for this reduction since the 1960s and 1970s has been not to stop greenhouse emissions, but to lessen air pollution. Burning coal releases not only CO_2 and methane, but also non-greenhouse gases, such as sulphur dioxide. These pollute the atmosphere, causing breathing difficulties and other health problems.

Evidence

THE WORLD'S FAVOURITE MATERIAL

Emissions are released when raw materials are made into building materials, from aluminium and glass to concrete and plastic. Concrete is probably the world's most commonly used material. Its production is responsible for nearly 5 per cent of all CO_2 made by human activities. During concrete manufacture, coal is burned to heat limestone and other ingredients to over 1,500 degrees Celsius. In the process, limestone reacts to release even more CO_2.

▲ This large area of tropical rainforest in Brazil has been cleared to create space for oil drilling.

Land-Use Change

The second biggest human cause of greenhouse gas emissions is land-use change. Across the globe, habitats from forests to grassland are being cleared to grow crops or keep livestock on, to build on or to mine into. Deforestation is also driven by the demand for timber and other products made from wood, such as paper. People cut down or log trees but also start fires in forests to remove trees or clear up logging waste, such as tree stumps and branches. Burning the waste releases a lot of CO_2. Bacteria in soil also emit CO_2 and methane when they break down the remaining tree waste. Farming on cleared land creates emissions, too. Livestock produce vast amounts of methane when they digest food. What is more, fertilisers put onto damaged soil to make it more fertile release nitrous oxide, which is 33 times worse than CO_2 as a greenhouse gas.

Absorbing Less

Land-use change has a double effect on the atmosphere. Apart from causing emissions, it reduces the absorption of carbon. Deforestation destroys forests, which are major carbon absorbers. Livestock trample the newly cleared soil on which they graze, damaging living things in soil that absorb CO_2.

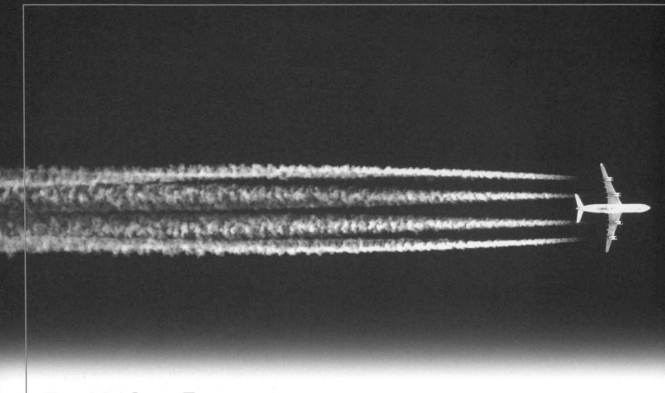

Trouble from Transport

At present, emissions from cars, trucks, ships and planes contribute about one-tenth of all the greenhouse gases produced by human activities. This proportion is growing annually. Between 1990 and 2000, emissions from transport increased by one-third because people were travelling more and because of global trade in transported goods. More and more people own cars each year. They use them to drive increasing total distances, often made up of shorter journeys to shops and work. Shorter journeys emit more greenhouse gas per kilometre than longer journeys because engines burn fuel less efficiently when they have not warmed up properly.

Total emissions from aeroplanes are increasing too because people are taking more flights. This is because flights are becoming cheaper and more goods are transported using aeroplanes as it is quicker than doing so by ship or road. In 2004, people worldwide took 3.9 billion flights, but transport experts predict that this number will double by 2020.

IT'S A FACT

- About 92 per cent of US households own at least one car.

- Cars and trucks accounted for 70 per cent of transport emissions in 2003.

- Based on fuel used at airports in the United Kingdom, emissions by aeroplanes doubled from 1990 to 2007.

◀ Contrails are trails of ice that form from water vapour released by aeroplane engines. The ice crystals add to high altitude-clouds that let sunlight through but stop heat moving from Earth to space.

Altitude Effects

The majority of emissions from aeroplanes happen high in the atmosphere. Greenhouse gases have up to twice the effect on climate the higher in the sky they are released. The reason is that the amount of energy a greenhouse gas molecule releases into the atmosphere depends on its temperature. At the altitudes at which aeroplanes fly, temperatures are below freezing. There cold molecules retain more heat and emit less into space.

Evidence

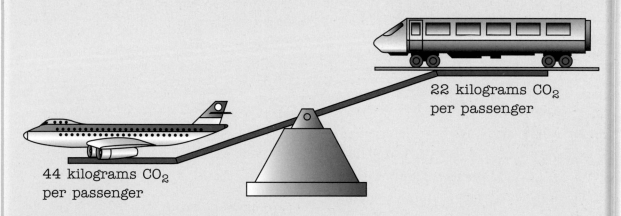

22 kilograms CO_2 per passenger

44 kilograms CO_2 per passenger

TRAINS VERSUS PLANES

Planes produce a lot of CO_2 for every kilometre travelled compared with other forms of transport. Scientists compared the emissions from the Eurostar train and aeroplanes going from London to Paris and back. They found out the number of people who travelled on the plane or train, how much fuel the plane used and how much fuel was needed to make the electricity the train used to move. They found that a train trip created just 10 per cent of the CO_2 emissions of an aeroplane flying the same journey. The journeys also took about the same time, when transfers to and from airports and waiting times at the airport were included in the calculation. In future, Eurostar may have an even smaller atmospheric impact as its developers plan to cut its emissions by a further 25 per cent.

Temperature Feedback

The way that various emissions affect climate is not straightforward. The gradual rise in greenhouse gases does not necessarily produce a gradual effect on the climate. The increasing heat that the gases store and emit can make the rate of climate change increase. The way in which products of a system feed into it and how they affect that system are described as feedback.

Some feedback happens at the Earth's surface, for example at ice sheets. Rising temperatures resulting from the greenhouse effect are melting ice. The albedo effect of ice normally reflects a lot of sunlight. However, once ice in one area melts it reveals darker

CASE STUDY
Shrinking Glacier

Jakobshavn glacier in Greenland, is a vast expanse of ice 6 kilometres wide and with a volume of 18 cubic kilometres. For the previous centuries the glacier has remained a fairly constant size. As new snow layers freeze onto the ice, the glacier flows towards the sea where it meets relatively warmer water, melts and breaks up into chunks of floating ice or icebergs. However, the glacier is now shrinking and moving faster than ever. In 2007, it melted twice as fast as during the last decade. The cause is feedback. Rising temperatures melt the glacier's surface, the meltwater drains between the ice and the rock underneath, and the glacier slips faster on the water.

▶ The upper edge of a glacier crashes into the ocean after its lower edge melts in seawater.

areas, such as rock or deep water, beneath. The dark areas absorb more sunlight, raising temperatures at the Earth's surface. The warming land melts ice around it more quickly. Then more heat is absorbed. The feedback speeds up climate change.

Greenhouse Gas Feedback

Slightly different feedback happens in the atmosphere with accelerating quantities of greenhouse gases. With rising surface temperatures, more water evaporates from lakes and oceans. The water vapour is a greenhouse gas that traps more heat, which evaporates more water. The hotter the land gets, the slower plants absorb CO_2 because photosynthesis slows. Therefore, CO_2 levels rise more. In the oceans, phytoplankton absorb less CO_2 because the gas dissolves less easily in the warming water.

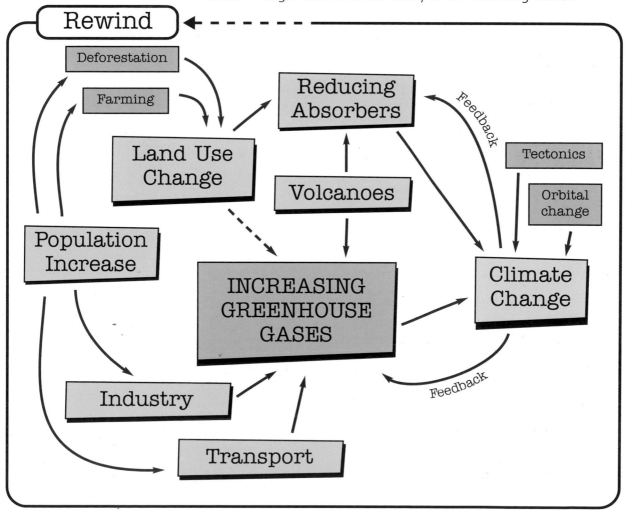

The Impact of Climate Change

Changing weather patterns and melting ice caps, which raise sea levels, are already having a wide range of impacts on people, other living things and the communities, habitats and biomes they inhabit. In future, if climate change increases, the impacts could be even greater.

The Prediction

Scientists around the world are studying how much climate is changing. They produce data on increasing greenhouse gas levels, how feedback is happening and what changing weather and temperature is doing to the distribution of life and natural resources on the planet. In February 2007, a group of scientists called the Intergovernmental Panel on Climate Change (IPCC) looked at all the data together and predicted the likely temperature rise by the end of the 21st century. The IPCC concluded that the most likely global average rise is 4 degrees Celsius but that it could be as much as 6.4 degrees Celsius.

Evidence

SEA LEVEL FORECAST

This graph shows the predicted sea-level rise for the future. Scientists made complicated calculations using data on emissions, how long greenhouse gases continue to warm the atmosphere, and knowledge about heat distribution and glacier thickness all around the world, for example. The further into the future they predict, the less certain the scientists become.

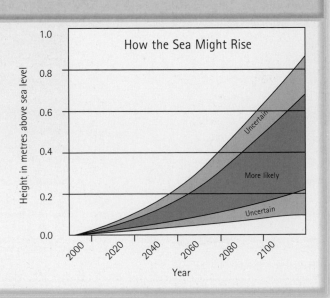

How the Sea Might Rise

Sea Change

The global temperature rise is causing sea-level rise. The rise is caused not only by a greater volume of water in the oceans due to ice melting, but also by the water getting warmer and less dense. Warm water molecules jiggle around more than cold molecules, so they take up more space. Warming at the Poles is gradually melting glaciers and ice sheets. It is often thought that the volume of meltwater from land would not be that great given the enormous amount of water already in the oceans. However, the average sea level rose by 15 centimetres in the 20th century and scientists estimate that by 2100, there could be a further rise of between 9 and 88 centimetres with an average of nearly 50 centimetres.

Effects of Rising Sea Levels

Globally about 100 million people live within 1 metre of sea level. They live on islands such as the Maldives in the Indian ocean and Tuvalu in the Pacific ocean, and in settlements in Bangladesh, India, West Africa and China. In these places, sea level rise would flood land with seawater. It would cover roads, buildings and industries such as ports, and contaminate freshwater supplies and soil. This would reduce water supplies and make land unsuitable for growing crops. Even without direct inundation, the higher level of water would be more easily pushed onto land by storm waves caused by winds. Storm surges of water can add 5 metres to the average sea level. High sea levels could also more easily erode or wear away coastal land. Changing salinity or saltiness of water owing to added meltwater from freshwater ice could gradually affect ocean currents. These play a big part in heat circulation around the globe.

▼ Settlements built at sea level are at most risk from sea level rise.

Changing Rainfall Patterns

Rising temperatures are already changing rainfall patterns. Increased evaporation of surface water is producing moister air. In the atmosphere over the oceans, there has been a 1 per cent increase in water vapour each decade. The water vapour is a greenhouse gas helping to trap heat and warm air masses. Increasing differences in temperature, and therefore pressure, of air masses cause stronger winds, shifting moist air masses through the atmosphere.

Too Much, Too Little

The redistribution of water is increasing the intensity of precipitation in some areas. Extreme bursts of heavy rain over short periods are becoming more common than longer periods

▲ The awesome forces of extreme weather affect LEDCs and MEDCs. Hurricane Katrina destroyed large parts of the big city of New Orleans, USA, in 2005.

of gentle rain in some areas. This can cause destructive floods and mudslides. Flooding affected 1.5 billion people, nearly a quarter of the world's population, between 1990 and 2001. Rising temperatures are also increasing the incidence of drought in other parts of the world. Areas such as the subtropical regions, including North Africa and Australia, are drying because so much water is evaporating.

Extreme Heat Effects

Extreme heat is a much bigger killer than drought, flooding, mudslides and strong winds put together. The worst heatwave on record was in Europe in 2003, when about 35,000 people died. High daytime temperatures combined with warmer-than-usual nights so that heat built up. The land did not cool overnight because water vapour that evaporated from the warm land trapped heat in the air. Many people died from overheating, but others from breathing difficulties caused by air pollution because the days were not only hot but also still, so winds did not blow away polluted air.

Heatwaves are not the only consequence of extreme heat. Extreme heat over the oceans is creating the right conditions for the strongest hurricanes. Hurricanes are powerful, rotating storms that form over very warm water masses. They cause greatest destruction when they blow off the sea and over coastal land. The projected rise in average global temperature through the 21st century could increase the number of category four and five hurricanes by about one-fifth.

CASE STUDY
Antarctica Cooling?

Not everywhere on Earth is getting warmer. The coldest, central part of Antarctica was cooler between 1966 and 2000 by 0.2 degrees Celsius each decade. This is because warmer air in the atmosphere above the continent has caused stronger winds blowing around and down onto Antarctica, rather like a whirlpool. This Antarctic vortex holds more cold air over the land and brings down freezing air from high in the atmosphere. As temperatures warm slightly, there will be more snow, adding thicker layers of ice to central Antarctica. However, the warming will cause further ice loss at places around the coasts of Antarctica.

Biome Shift

Many living things can cope with changing climate by moving to or growing in new areas where the climate has become suitable for them. Scientists studied 99 species, including birds, butterflies and mountain plants, in North America and Europe. They worked out that on average, the limits of the areas they could live in had shifted northward by 6.1 kilometres, or upward to higher altitudes by 6.1 metres per decade. Many were also breeding earlier in the year because the temperate climate was warmer.

Other animals cannot cope with climate change even though they can move. For example, the eggs of many beach-nesting turtles hatch more females than males when the temperature of the sand is warmer. Climate change could make their breeding difficult as individuals cannot find mates. Many coral species cannot grow so well in the changing climate because the increasing amount of CO_2 dissolved in the oceans is making the water too acidic. This makes it more difficult for them to build the reefs where their colonies live.

▼ Apollo butterflies are threatened because they have less and less mountain habitat in which to live. This is because temperatures on lower slopes are too warm for them, so they have to live higher up mountains to survive.

ANT ATTACK!

The red fire ant is a destructive pest from South America that was imported accidentally into the southern United States. Fire ants die if nights are very cold, but warmer nights resulting from climate change are allowing them to spread northward. The ants are increasing their territory each year by the size of the state of New Hampshire. When the ants build their large nest mounds, they damage plant roots in gardens and fields. The ants feed largely on plants but will sometimes kill anything from bees to lizards to eat.

The major problem people have with these ants is their aggression. The fire ants inflict painful, sometimes serious, stings on people, their pets, livestock and other animals. The ants are also attracted to the buzzing of electrical equipment, such as traffic lights. They sting the wire, stopping the lights from working and potentially causing serious accidents.

About US$5 billion is spent each year in the United States on medical treatment and repairing damage caused by fire ants and on the destruction of the ants.

Spreading Disease

Climate affects the spread of disease-causing organisms, or pathogens, and the animals that carry them. For example, the ticks that spread Lyme disease pathogens live on the blood of deer, sheep and cattle. They bite people who move through the areas where these animals live and pass on the pathogens. Lyme disease causes long-term disability and is increasing in the United Kingdom and North America because ticks increase in numbers when winters are not cold enough to kill them.

Mosquitoes spread malaria, yellow fever, and other diseases that kill hundreds of thousands of people worldwide annually. Mosquitoes grow faster in warming climates. They breed in puddles and ponds that increase after floods and reduce after droughts. However, both droughts and floods force poor people in LEDCs to drink dirty water containing pathogens causing diseases such as typhoid or cholera. In a drought, people may have only dirty water to drink, and floodwater after rains may wash pathogens into clean water supplies.

Climate and Crops

Climate change is having good and bad impacts on crops. Increased temperatures damage some crops, for example lettuces are easily scorched. However, warming of the air prolongs the growing seasons of many crops, such as strawberries, and increases the choice of crops that can be grown in many areas. Increased CO_2 makes crops grow faster, because the plants use it to make their food during photosynthesis. However, each plant is smaller and produces fewer nutrients when there is more CO_2 in the air.

Warmer conditions are allowing the spread of crop pests. For example, potato farming in United Kingdom would be at risk if Colorado beetles, which eat the plants, spread from mainland Europe, where it is currently warmer than in the United Kingdom. Drought conditions can also make crops fail. Scientists estimate that by the end of the 21st century, there could be a global average fall in food production of around one-tenth owing to drying cropland. In some parts of Africa the loss could be over one-third.

Evidence

FACE-ING THE FUTURE

Since 1990, scientists have been carrying out Free Air Carbon dioxide Enrichment (FACE) experiments. In the experiments, the scientists grow crops in enclosed spaces containing air with higher CO_2 concentrations than normal. They then compare the size, weight, and number of seeds or fruit on each plant to check whether atmospheric change in future will affect the yield of food crops. Results from the experiments show that crop plants have greater yields with increased proportions of atmospheric CO_2, so long as the soil conditions are dry. This could mean that future drought conditions in some croplands may not prevent food being grown there.

▼ The wheat belt, or area where wheat plants grow best in North America, is shifting northwards from the United States towards Canada as climate changes.

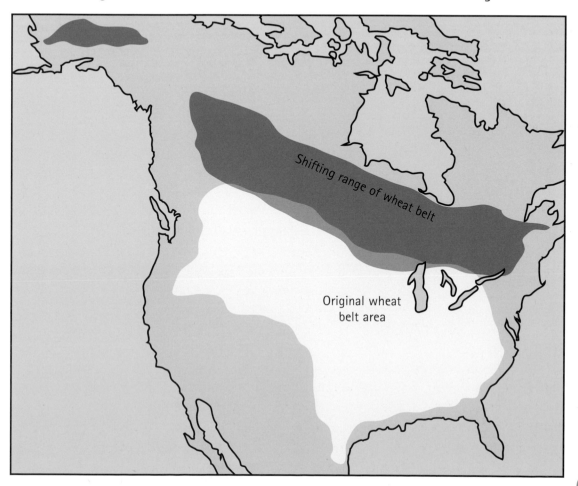

Shifting range of wheat belt

Original wheat belt area

No one can hide from climate change!

The Camp for Climate Action

Head down to Megawatt Valley (near Leeds) for 10 days of action, information and discussion to stop climate chaos.

26th Aug – 4th Sept 2006
www.climatecamp.org.uk

Water Supply

Changing rainfall patterns will affect water supply. For example, shrinking glaciers in mountain ranges such as the Andes, Rockies and Himalayas are increasing the flow of meltwater. In Nepal and neighbouring Bhutan, more than 40 mountain lakes are filling so rapidly they could overflow and cause major flooding within the next decade. River water is critical for domestic supply, irrigation of crops, hydroelectric power, industry and many other uses. The rivers Indus and Ganges get nearly all their water, supplying half a billion people, from glaciers in Nepal and other Himalayan countries. However, while river levels are rising in the warming months after winter, they are falling during warmer summers. And as glaciers are shrinking, their long-term supply of meltwater is limited. All of these factors make water supply uncertain.

More sporadic and intense rainfall is causing runoff and failing to top up overused groundwater reserves. Digging deeper to find more groundwater causes further problems. It brings salts from underground rocks to the surface. The salty water can damage crops when used for irrigation and spoil drinking water supplies. Inundation of salt water resulting from rising sea levels also spoils freshwater resources.

Migration

The impact of climate change on the supply of resources such as fresh water and food is causing changes to human distribution across the globe. The projected rise in average temperature could force one in seven people to migrate over the next 50 years.

▲ The Camp for Climate Action is one of many groups taking action to publicise the dangers of increasing greenhouse gas emissions.

People will be worse affected north and south of the Sahara and in the Middle East, where water and good cropland is in short supply. People often migrate to large cities in the hope of finding work. This movement will increase already large populations, putting pressure on water supplies, housing and other resources.

Conflict

Spreading desert lands, resulting in part from climate change, are already increasing conflicts in different parts of the world. For example, tensions between communities in Ghana, and between Israel and Palestine are caused in part by conflict over dwindling water resources. There is also conflict between groups who encourage or oppose industrialisation, increased transport, tourism and other development of regions and countries. For example, many of those taking part in large-scale protests about a new London airport in the United Kingdom in 2007 were motivated by fears about greenhouse gas emissions from increased numbers of aircraft.

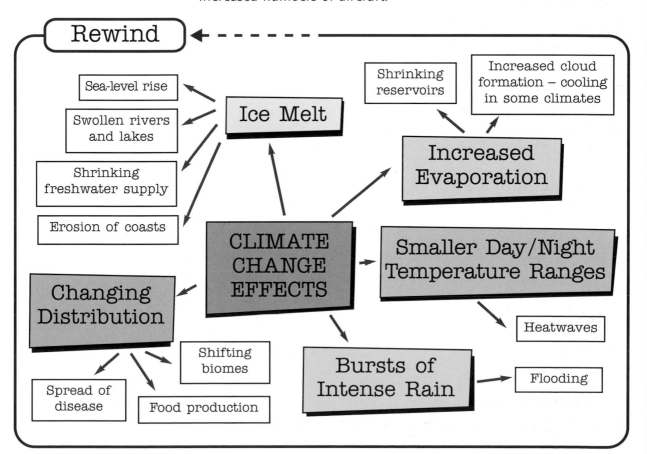

Rewind

Sea-level rise

Swollen rivers and lakes

Shrinking freshwater supply

Erosion of coasts

Ice Melt

Shrinking reservoirs

Increased cloud formation – cooling in some climates

Increased Evaporation

CLIMATE CHANGE EFFECTS

Smaller Day/Night Temperature Ranges

Heatwaves

Changing Distribution

Shifting biomes

Spread of disease

Food production

Bursts of Intense Rain

Flooding

Sustainable Solutions

As people have caused rapid climate change by how they live, so they can use different solutions to reduce emissions. To make solutions last into the future, everyone, from individuals to governments, needs to take responsibility for their effect on the planet.

Lifestyle Choices

Lifestyle affects greenhouse gas emissions. Someone who cycles to work is responsible for fewer emissions from transport than someone who drives to work. People can choose to reduce energy usage, such as boiling only the water needed for a cup of tea rather than a full kettle. People can also buy locally produced food rather than that which is transported for long distances, or even flown in from other countries. Technology can also help people to make choices. For example, using efficient solar ovens rather than normal fires to cook with helps to protect tropical trees from being chopped down for fuelwood. However, poor people in LEDCs may have little option to change their lifestyle to help the atmosphere. For example, rice is the staple food for about one-third of the world's population. Rice farmers must flood fields to grow their crops, but this releases methane. Reducing rice farming to reduce emissions could damage food supply.

▼ In those places with the right weather conditions, wind is a plentiful, free and sustainable energy resource.

Different Power

Reducing overall power usage is tricky in a world where electric gadgets and transport are on the rise. Many governments and individuals are promoting the use of sustainable energy sources. Something that is sustainable has no harmful effect on the planet. Solar, wind, hydro and wave power use sunlight, moving air, falling water and wave forces as energy sources. Unlike fossil fuels, these sources are in endless supply and produce no greenhouse gas emissions.

Biofuels are sustainable alternatives to the petrol and diesel used in vehicles. They are processed from fast-growing crops including palm oil and maize, or from food or crop waste. The trouble with biofuels is that CO_2 emissions are produced during processing and when they are burned. What is more, biofuels are in demand and fetch a good price, so people in tropical LEDCs may deforest land purely to grow them.

CASE STUDY
New Oil

The jatropha bush is a poisonous plant whose abundant seeds are traditionally used to relieve constipation. It has recently been discovered that the seeds can also be processed into oil for use in engines. Just 1 hectare of land can produce 2.7 tonnes of oil, and the waste from processing can be burned to release energy, too. Jatropha is drought-tolerant and grows easily in dry wasteland that cannot be farmed for food crops. Mali, in West Africa, hopes to power 12,000 villages using jatropha grown on its poor soils.

▶ Growing jatropha plants is one sustainable solution to dwindling oil supplies. But burning this fuel still creates emissions.

Cleaning Up

One solution for reducing emissions is to clean up the power technology that is already used. Increasing numbers of chimneys on factories are fitted with scrubbers, which are special filters that remove greenhouse gases from smoke. Scientists are researching how to pump greenhouse gases into empty underground spaces, such as those from which oil or gas was removed under oceans. This is called carbon capture and storage, or CCS. An advantage of CCS over sustainable energy technologies is that it is an add-on to existing industries using fossil fuels. The disadvantages are that the technology might not work in the long run and that building pipes to carry the gases will be expensive, making the cost of electricity higher.

Growing Sinks

Forests and phytoplankton are often described as carbon sinks because they absorb CO_2 from the atmosphere. People can easily increase the forest sink by stopping deforestation and planting trees. In 2007, there was a global campaign to plant a billion new trees during the year. The many added benefits of planting trees include reducing land erosion, as tree roots hold together soil, and increasing the number and range of organisms in the forest biome. Scientists are also looking at ways to increase numbers of phytoplankton and create a larger oceanic carbon sink.

Changing the Atmosphere

Another solution to climate change is to use technology to reduce temperatures without reducing greenhouse gas emissions. Some scientists believe that the way to do this is by firing sulphur dioxide into the atmosphere. The gas would form droplets of sulphate that reflect sunlight back into space and cool the Earth. There are many problems with this idea. One is that CO_2 would still be building up and possibly making the oceans too acidic for plankton. It is uncertain what effect sulphur dioxide could have on the climate system, too.

CASE STUDY
Ironing out Carbon

People are testing how fertilising small patches of ocean with iron sulphate can make more phytoplankton grow and increase the oceanic carbon sink. Iron found in this chemical is a vital nutrient that increases growth and reproduction in phytolankton populations. The more phytoplankton plants there are, the greater the amount of CO_2 that is removed from the atmosphere through photosynthesis. If the tests are successful in lowering CO_2, widespread ocean fertilisation may begin, especially in areas where plankton numbers are low.

The long-term hope is to lower global temperatures. Some scientists have analysed the iron and phytoplankton content of rocks formed at the bottom of oceans and concluded that there is a link between global temperature and iron. They believe that past ice ages may have followed periods when a lot of iron from land got into the oceans. However, others foresee problems. Once phytoplankton dies, some of it sinks to the deep ocean floor taking carbon with it, but other phytoplankton are decomposed at the ocean surface releasing CO_2. Also, large masses of plankton can release methane, which is a more harmful greenhouse gas than CO_2.

▼ Up to 100 phytoplankton end to end measure just 1 millimetre. These tiny organisms drift or swim through the world's oceans.

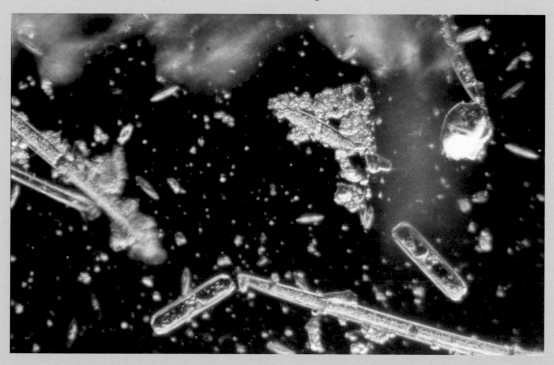

Working Together

Climate change is a global problem, so countries need to work together to help the atmosphere. In 1992, the United Nations (UN) met in Rio, Brazil, and agreed the link between emissions, mostly from MEDCs, and increasing temperatures. In 1997, another meeting was held in Japan, this time to agree how much individual countries could reasonably emit based on factors such as population and level of industrial development. This was the Kyoto Protocol. Scientists then worked out targets for reducing emissions.

Emission Impossible?

Most countries have adopted the Kyoto Protocol. Their emissions targets differ, but on average they are aiming to reduce their emissions by 5 per cent of their 1990 levels by 2012. However, even if Kyoto targets are met, they are only the initial steps in reducing emissions. Scientists estimate that a 60–80 per cent reduction by 2050 is needed to avert significant and rapid climate change.

Some countries, including the United States and Australia, have not signed the Kyoto Protocol. These countries are responsible for over one-third of global greenhouse gas emissions. The United States, for example, objected that the Protocol did not demand emissions reductions from LEDCs and was therefore unfair. However, like many other countries, the United States has its own emissions targets.

▶ Since 2003, people have had to pay a congestion charge to drive cars into the centre of London, England. The charge helps to fund the existing public transport system whilst reducing the traffic in the city. Greenhouse gas emissions in the zone have been cut by 19 per cent.

Evidence

CUTTING EMISSIONS

This pie chart shows the range of emission projects from 2004–2005.

The percentages are out of the total CO_2 and other greenhouse gases prevented from entering the atmosphere.

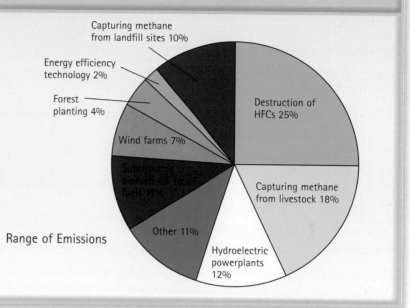

Capturing methane from landfill sites 10%

Energy efficiency technology 2%

Forest planting 4%

Destruction of HFCs 25%

Wind farms 7%

Substitution of biofuels for fossil fuels 11%

Capturing methane from livestock 18%

Other 11%

Hydroelectric powerplants 12%

Range of Emissions

Sharing the Credit

Many countries are struggling to reduce their emissions. One way they help to meet their targets is by buying carbon credits. Imagine one country emitted ten units of CO_2 more than its target and another country emitted ten less. The first country could pay the second for its CO_2 allocation by buying carbon credits.

Over half of all the carbon credits earned from emission reduction projects come from just six massive projects. All of these projects are based in factories in India, China and South Korea that make chemicals called refrigerants that keep refrigerators cool. A byproduct of making refrigerants is HFC, which is the most powerful greenhouse gas. The factories install special burners to get rid of the HFC. MEDCs pay for the companies to burn amounts of HFC in exchange for carbon credits. The factories make lots of money from selling credits and the atmosphere has fewer greenhouse gases. But there are some problems with this system. Burning destroys HFC but also releases polluting non-greenhouse gases into the atmosphere that can damage health. In addition, some factories produce far more refrigerant than they need to sell, purely to make more HFC that they can then burn for profit.

Investing in Credits

Another way a country can gain credits is by investing in new projects committed to reducing greenhouse gases, such as tree-planting projects. One of the advantages of this system is that many projects happen in LEDCs and help poor people. However, carbon credits can be awarded even if development is unsustainable or polluting. For example, a Brazilian steel factory used plantation-grown wood to make charcoal, rather than more-polluting coal. However, to do this they cut down a section of rainforest to make way for the plantation.

Balancing Act

Balancing emissions that a company or individual is responsible for with reductions or savings in emissions elsewhere, is often called offsetting. Critics of offsetting say that it is a cop out and that anyone can make energy savings if they want to. Offsetting should be used only as a last resort. However, offsetting can be essential for some organisations.

CASE STUDY
Green Gherkin

Office buildings use up a lot of power in lighting and heating, so architects are finding more sustainable energy solutions. The Swiss Re building, or gherkin, in London is the United Kingdom's first environmentally progressive high-rise building. Its advanced double-glazed skin protects the inside from getting too hot or cold in different weather. The space inside has numerous tunnels or shafts between the floors, allowing air to flow through the inside. This reduces the cost of air conditioning and heating by around 40 per cent over similarly sized buildings.

► The gherkin has a bold design inside and out.

Governments often tell large individual companies in their countries how much they can emit and the companies may have to offset if they go over that limit. For example, a power company with fossil fuel powerplants may emit over the limit in order to make the power it needs to sell to stay in business. It might be too expensive to convert those powerplants to use sustainable fuels or to develop power from renewable energy. A cheaper option is to offset their emissions by buying carbon credits.

Responsible Offsetting

Many companies and individuals choose to offset because they understand and care about the issue of climate change. They may already be trying to reduce the emissions they are responsible for as much as they can, but acknowledge that some of their activities have an impact on the atmosphere. For example, someone taking a flight on holiday can pay a company to plant trees on their behalf. The number of trees planted depends on the distance travelled. Generally, more gas is emitted the more kilometres travelled, so long-haul holidays will cost more to offset than shorter trips.

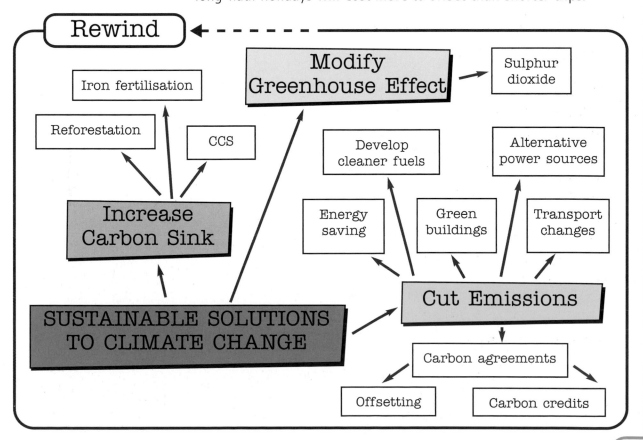

What the Future Holds

Whether or not the Earth can cope with climate change depends on the choices people make. Right now they have the opportunity to make a real difference to the planet. Doing nothing and carrying on as they have through the last century will only make problems worse.

Possible Future

An unregulated increase in transport and industry in LEDCs could make their cumulative emissions reach those of MEDCs by the end of the 21st century. By then, increasing temperatures could have affected sea levels and weather, food supply and migration. The IPCC predicts that by 2080, about 2 billion people might not have enough water, 7 million people around coasts could be flooded and over half a billion could be hungry as a result of climate change. Emissions could snowball because of feedback. For example, a frozen Siberian bog the size of France and Germany combined could be completely thawed out for first time in 11,000 years, releasing billions of tonnes of methane. Political problems owing to the effects of climate change on society could make international emission reductions even more difficult to agree on.

▼ The disappearing Arctic could mean a leap into the unknown for future populations of polar bears and other organisms adapted to life on the ice caps.

Evidence

LASTING EFFECTS

Many scientists predict that if emissions are reduced after 2050, greenhouse gases in the atmosphere will continue to rise into the next century before stabilising. However, temperature will continue to rise slightly and feedback effects will make sea levels rise for centuries.

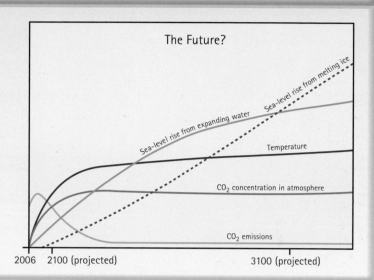

The Future?

Sea-level rise from expanding water

Sea-level rise from melting ice

Temperature

CO_2 concentration in atmosphere

CO_2 emissions

2006   2100 (projected)   3100 (projected)

A Question of Scales

Some scientists argue that the evidence for climate change becomes less clear when longer timescales are examined. They say that the fast warming over the last century is just one 'up' amongst many 'ups and downs' in temperature over tens of thousands of years, during the gradual warming of Earth since the last ice age. However, this gradual warming is just part of a general cooling of Earth over tens of millions of years. In future, people may not bother to cut emissions if they feel assured by this view of Earth's temperature history.

Doing the Carbon Sums

One of the biggest mistakes over the last century, especially in MEDCs, has been ignoring the impact on climate of greenhouse gas emissions produced during industrial development. Governments, businesses and individuals need to take responsibility for the emissions that they produce by doing carbon sums. Most products today have a carbon footprint. This is a measure of the amount of CO_2 they are responsible for. For example, locally produced tomatoes usually have a much smaller footprint than tomatoes grown in a distant country.

CASE STUDY
Changes in China

There is a massive industrial revolution happening in China. Chinese factories now make a large proportion of the manufactured goods bought in the United States, Japan and Europe.

To provide enough power, China is building about two power stations every week, causing soaring emissions. In 2006, China's CO_2 emissions rose by 9 per cent. Some people claim that China will soon emit more greenhouse gases than any other single country. However, the average emissions per person in the Chinese population are still much lower than an average person from an MEDC.

▼ This is an artist's impression of Dongtan ecocity, planned near Shanghai, which is designed to reduce emissions.

Some people argue that most of China's emissions are the fault of MEDCs whose companies can make products more cheaply in Chinese factories.

China has no emissions targets, even though it signed the Kyoto protocol. It argues that as a developing country it should be excused, partly as its emissions have been happening only from the end of the 20th century, whereas emissions from MEDCs have been building up in the atmosphere for over 150 years. Nevertheless, China has an ambitous national plan to help combat climate change. It aims to:
• Increase industrial efficiency by 20 per cent by 2010;
• Increase use of less polluting fuels;
• Increase forest cover;
• Invest in energy-saving technology;
• Educate people to save energy.

A Preferable Future

Many people believe that decisive action will achieve a preferable future of much slower climate change. Some of the types of action that will make a real difference include doubling how far cars can travel per litre of fuel and halving the distance each car drives: this will require development of better engines for cars, taking more shared trips and using public transport more. Wind power and solar power can be expanded to replace coal as a fuel source: this would require a total area the size of Germany. By using CCS, developing new carbon sinks and halting deforestation, CO_2 levels could drop.

Spreading the Word

Governments can do only so much to spread the word about climate change. Charities, scientific groups and the involvement of high-profile people are also important in keeping people informed about the problems and also putting pressure on governments to act. Charities working towards reducing emissions include the Natural Resources Defense Council and Friends of the Earth. Ex-US Vice President Al Gore and the IPCC were awarded the Nobel Peace Prize for their part in providing information and globally promoting the dangers of climate change.

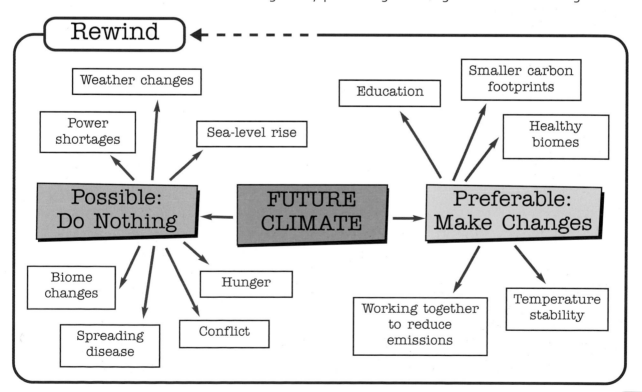

Glossary and Further Information

Albedo The light and warmth reflectivity of surfaces.

Aspect The lie of the land, such as slope steepness.

Biome An environment with a characteristic community of living things determined largely by climate.

CCS (Carbon Capture and Storage) A system of removing CO_2 from factory and power station emissions and storing it underground.

Carbon credit A way of giving carbon emissions a value that can be traded.

Carbon footprint A measure of the quantity of emissions caused by an activity or the manufacture of a product.

Carbon sink A place that absorbs more CO_2 than it produces, such as a forest or ocean.

Continental drift The change in position of land masses owing to movement of plates in the Earth's outer crust.

Deforestation Cutting down or burning down large areas of trees

Glacier A moving river of ice.

Greenhouse gases The gases in the atmosphere that keep Earth warm by absorbing the Sun's heat.

Groundwater Water that collects or flows deep underground.

Ice age A period of extremely low temperatures with widespread ice sheets.

Ice sheet A thick expanse of ice covering the Earth's surface.

Monsoon Wind laden with water vapour that blows from warm seas over cooler land, bringing rain.

Orbit The path of one object moving around another.

Pathogen A disease-causing organism.

Permafrost A frozen layer of soil.

Phytoplankton Plant-like organisms found mostly in oceans.

Sustainable When resource use meets present needs without harming future resource needs.

Log On

http://.epa.gov/climatechange/kids/index.html
This website has information on all aspects of global warming.

www.panda.org/about_wwf/what_we_do/climate_change/index.cfm
The WWF's website looks at climate change and how everyone can make a difference.

www.worldviewofglobalwarming.org
Every picture tells a story: this website shows the effect of climate change through photography.

Visit

The Eden Project
The plastic domes at the Eden Project in Cornwall, England, house a variety of world biomes. There are plans to extend the current space devoted to climate change. For more information, go to
www.edenproject.com

Read

Changing Climate: Living with the Weather, Louise Spilsbury (Raintree 2006)

An Inconvenient Truth: The Crisis of Global Warming, Al Gore (Viking, 2007)

National Geographic Investigates Extreme Weather: Science Tackles Global Warming and Climate Change, Kathleen Simpson (National Geographic, 2008)

Topic Web

Use this topic web to discover themes and ideas in subjects that are related to climate change.

English and Literacy

- Imagine what the climate will be like in 50 years time. Write a story about the life of your imaginary grandchild in that future.
- Read newspaper accounts of people forced to move or who are otherwise affected by flooding, drought and other problems that may be the result of global warming.

Science and Environment

- Contrast the effects of climate change on food webs in the Arctic and grassland biomes.
- Research the importance of coral reefs for ocean biodiversity and the signs of climate change in coral populations.
- Draw up a list of measures that your school could take to reduce power usage.

Geography

- Examine the greenhouse gas emissions by a country or continent; how do MEDCs and LEDCs compare?
- Research how Antarctica will be affected by climate change and the effect this might have on access to its mineral resources.

History and Economics

- Look at the changes in the transport, agriculture and production industries from the Industrial Revolution to today.
- Research the roles played by individuals in climate change, such as the inventor of the steam engine or major climate change protestors.
- Review the development of renewable energy resources in the 20th century and the effect of changes in the price of oil.

Climate Change

Art and Culture

- Design a poster to communicate the threats of climate change using images found using a web browser.
- Films about climate change, such as *The Day After Tomorrow* imagine future worlds and raise awareness of environmental issues. Script your own short film about climate change.

Index